A PLEA FOR ATHEISM.

———
———

BY C. BRADLAUGH.

GILLESPIE says that "an Atheist propagandist seems a nondescript monster created by nature in a moment of madness." Despite this opinion, it is as the propagandist of Atheism that I pen the following lines, in the hope that I may succeed in removing some few of the many prejudices which have been created against not only the actual holders of Atheistic opinions, but also against those wrongfully suspected of entertaining such ideas. Men who have been famous for depth of thought, for excellent wit, or great genius, have been recklessly assailed as Atheists, by those who lacked the high qualifications against which the spleen of the calumniators was directed. Thus, not only has Voltaire been without ground accused of Atheism, but Bacon, Locke, and Bishop Berkeley himself, have, amongst others, been denounced by thoughtless or unscrupulous pietists as inclining to Atheism, the ground for the accusation being that they manifested an inclination to improve human thought.

It is too often the fashion with persons of pious reputation to speak in unmeasured language of Atheism as favouring immorality, and of Atheists as men whose conduct is necessarily vicious, and who have adopted atheistic views as a desperate defiance against a Deity justly offended by the badness of their lives. Such persons urge that amongst the proximate causes of Atheism are vicious training, immoral and profligate companions, licentious living, and the like. Dr. **John Pye Smith**, in his "**Instructions on Christian Theology**," goes so far as to declare that "nearly all the Atheists upon record have been men of extremely debauched and vile conduct." Such language from the Christian advocate is not surprising, but there are others who, professing great desire for the spread of Freethought, and with pretensions to rank amongst acute and liberal thinkers, declare Atheism impracticable, and its teachings cold, barren, and negative. In this brief essay I shall except to each of the above allegations, and shall endeavour to demonstrate that Atheism affords greater possibility for human happiness than any system yet based on Theism, or possible to be founded thereon, and that the lives of true Atheists must be more virtuous, because more human, than those of the believers in Deity, the humanity of the devout believer often finding itself neutralised by a faith with which it is necessarily in constant collision. The devotee piling the faggots at the *auto da fé* of an heretic, and that heretic his son, might, notwithstanding, be a good father in every respect but this. Heresy, in the eyes of the believer, is highest criminality, and outweighs all claims of family or affection.

Atheism, properly understood, is in nowise a cold, barren negative; it is, on the contrary, a hearty, fruitful affirmation of all truth, and involves the positive assertion and action of highest humanity.

Let Atheism be fairly examined, and neither condemned—its defence unheard—on the *ex parte* slanders of the professional preachers of fashionable orthodoxy, whose courage is bold enough while the pulpit protects the sermon, but whose valour becomes tempered with discretion when a free platform is afforded and discussion claimed; nor misjudged because it has been the custom to regard Atheism as so unpopular as to render its advocacy impolitic. The best policy against all prejudice is to assert firmly the verity. The Atheist does not say "There is no God," but he says, "I know not what you mean by God; I am without idea of God; the word 'God' is to me a sound conveying no clear or distinct affirmation. I do not deny God, because I cannot deny that of which I have no conception, and the conception of which, by its affirmer, is so imperfect that he is unable to define it to me." If you speak to the Atheist of God as creator, he answers that the conception of creation is impossible. We are utterly unable to construe it in thought as possible that the complement of existence has been either increased or diminished, much less can we conceive an absolute origination of substance. We cannot conceive either, on the one hand, nothing becoming something, or on the other, something becoming nothing. The Theist who speaks of God creating the universe, must either suppose that Deity evolved it out of himself, or that he produced it from nothing. But the Theist cannot regard the universe as evolution of Deity, because this would identify Universe and Deity, and be Pantheism rather than Theism. There would be no distinction of substance—in fact no creation. Nor can the Theist regard the universe as created out of nothing, because Deity is, according to him, necessarily eternal and infinite. His existence being eternal and infinite, precludes the possibility of the conception of vacuum to be filled by the universe if created. No one can even think of any point of existence in extent or duration and say, here is the point of separation between the creator and the created. Indeed, it is not possible for the Theist to imagine a beginning to the universe. It is not possible to conceive either an absolute commencement, or an absolute termination of existence; that is, it is impossible to conceive beginning before which you have a period when the universe has yet to be; or to conceive an end, after which the universe, having been, no longer exists. It is impossible in thought to originate or annihilate the universe. The Atheist affirms that he cognises to-day effects, that these are at the same time causes and effects—causes to the effects they precede, effects to the causes they follow. Cause is simply everything without which the effect would not result, and with which it must result. Cause is the means to an end, consummating itself in that end. The Theist who argues for creation must assert a point of time, that is, of duration, when the created did not yet exist. At this point of time either something existed or nothing; but something must have existed, for out of nothing nothing can come. Something must have existed, because the point fixed upon is that of the duration of something. This something must have been either finite or infinite; it finite, it could not have been God, and if the something were infinite, then creation was impossible, as it is impossible to add to infinite existence.

If you leave the question of creation and deal with the government of the universe, the difficulties of Theism are by no means lessened. The existence of evil is then a terrible stumbling-block to the Theist. Pain, misery, crime, poverty, confront the advocate of eternal goodness, and challenge with unanswerable potency his declaration of Deity as all-good, all-wise, and all-powerful. Evil is either caused by God, or exists independently; but it cannot be caused by God, as in that case he would not be all-good; nor can it exist independently, as in that case he would not be all-powerful. Evil must either have had a beginning, or it must be eternal; but, according to the Theist, it cannot be eternal, because God alone is eternal. Nor can it have had a beginning, for if it had it must either have originated in God. or outside God; but, according to the Theist, it cannot have originated in God, for he is all-good, and out of all-goodness evil cannot originate; nor can evil have originated outside God, for, according to the Theist, God is infinite, and it is impossible to go outside of or beyond infinity.

To the Atheist this question of evil assumes an entirely different aspect. He declares that evil is a result, but not a result from God or Devil. He affirms that by conduct founded on knowledge of the laws of existence it is possible to ameliorate and avoid present evil, and, as our knowledge increases, to prevent its future recurrence.

Some declare that the belief in God is necessary as a check to crime. They allege that the Atheist may commit murder, lie, or steal without fear of any consequences. To try the actual value of this argument, it is not unfair to ask—Do Theists ever steal? If yes, then in each such theft, the belief in God and his power to punish has been inefficient as a preventive of the crime. Do Theists ever lie or murder? If yes, the same remark has further force—hell-fire failing against the lesser as against the greater crime. The fact is that those who use such an argument overlook a great truth—*i.e.*, that all men seek happiness, though in very diverse fashions.

Ignorant and miseducated men often mistake the true path to happiness, and commit crime in the endeavour to obtain it. Atheists hold that by teaching mankind the real road to human happiness, it is possible to keep them from the by-ways of criminality and error. Atheists would teach men to be moral now, not because God offers as an inducement reward by and by, but because in the virtuous act itself immediate good is ensured to the doer and the circle surrounding him. Atheism would preserve man from lying, stealing, murdering now, not from fear of an eternal agony after death, but because these crimes make this life itself a course of misery.

While Theism, asserting God as the creator and governor of the universe, hinders and checks man's efforts by declaring God's will to be the sole directing and controlling power, Atheism, by declaring all events to be in accordance with natural laws—that is, happening in certain ascertainable sequences—stimulates man to discover the best conditions of life, and offers him the most powerful inducements to morality. While the Theist provides future happiness for a scoundrel repentant on his death-bed, Atheism affirms present and certain happiness for the man who does his best to live here so well as to have little cause for repenting hereafter.

Theism declares that God dispenses health and inflicts disease, and sickness and illness are regarded by the Theist as visitations from an angered Deity, to be borne with meekness and content. Atheism declares that physiological knowledge may preserve us from disease by preventing our infringing the law of health, and that sickness results not as the ordinance of offended Deity, but from ill-ventilated dwellings and workshops, bad and insufficient food, excessive toil, mental suffering, exposure to inclement weather, and the like—all these finding root in poverty, the chief source of crime and disease; that prayers and piety afford no protection against fever, and that if the human being be kept without food he will starve as quickly whether he be Theist or Atheist, theology being no substitute for bread.

When the Theist ventures to affirm that his God is an existence other than and separate from the so-called material universe, and when he invests this separate, hypothetical existence with the several attributes of omniscience, omnipresence, omnipotence, eternity, infinity, immutability, and perfect goodness, then the Atheist, in reply, says—"I deny the existence of such a being."

It becomes very important, in order that injustice may not be done to the Theistic argument, that we should have—in lieu of a clear definition, which it seems useless to ask for—the best possible clue to the meaning intended to be conveyed by the word God. If it were not that the word is an arbitrary term, invented for the ignorant, and the notions suggested by which are vague and entirely contingent upon individual fancies, such a clue could be probably most easily and satisfactorily obtained by tracing back the word "God," and ascertaining the sense in which it was used by the uneducated worshippers who have gone before us; collating this with the more modern Theism, qualified as it is by the superior knowledge of to-day. Dupuis says—"Le mot

Dieu parâit destiné à exprimer l'idée de la force universelle et eternellement active qui imprime le mouvement à tout dans la Nature, suivant les lois d'une harmonie constant et admirable, qui se developpe dans les diverses formes que prend la matière organisée, qui se mêle à tout, anime tout, et qui semble être une dans ses modifications infiniment variées, et n'appartenir qu'à elle-même." "The word God appears intended to express the force universal, and eternally active, which endows all nature with motion according to the laws of a constant and admirable harmony; which develops itself in the diverse forms of organised matter, which mingles with all, gives life to all; which seems to be one through all its infinitely varied modifications, and inheres in itself alone."

In the "Bon Sens" of Curé Meslier, it is asked, "Qu'est-ce que Dieu?" and the answer is "C'est un mot abstrait fait pour designer la force cachée de la nature; ou c'est un point mathematique qui n'a ni longueur, ni largeur, ni profundeur." "It is an abstract word coined to designate the hidden force of nature, or rather it is a mathematical point having neither length, breadth, nor thickness."

The orthodox fringe of the Theism of to-day is Hebraistic in its origin—that is, it finds its root in the superstition and ignorance of a petty and barbarous people nearly destitute of literature, poor in language, and almost entirely wanting in high conceptions of humanity. It might, as Judaism is the foundation of Christianity, be fairly expected that the ancient Jewish Records would aid us in our search after the meaning to be attached to the word "God."

The most prominent words in Hebrew rendered God or Lord in English are יהוה *Jeue*, and אל'הים *Aleim*. The first word Jeue, called by our orthodox Jehovah, is equivalent to "that which exists," and indeed embodies in itself the only possible trinity in unity—*i.e.*, past, present, and future. There is nothing in this Hebrew word to help you to any such definition as is required for the sustenance of modern Theism. The most you can make of it by any stretch of imagination is equivalent to the declaration "I am, I have been,I shall be." The word יהוי is hardly ever spoken by the religious Jews who actually in reading substitute for it, Adonai, an entirely different word. Dr. Wall notices the close resemblance in sound between the word *Yehowa* or *Yeue*, or Jehovah, and Jove. In fact Ζεύς πατήρ Jupiter and Jeue—pater (God the father) present still closer resemblance in sound. Jove is also Ζεύς or θεὸς or Δεύς, whence the word Deus and our Deity. The Greek mythology, far more ancient than that of the Hebrews, has probably found for Christianity many other and more important features of coincidence than that of a similarly sounding name. The word θεὸς traced back affords us no help beyond that it identifies Deity with the universe. Plato says that the early Greeks thought that the only Gods (ΘΕΟΥΣ) were the sun, moon, earth, stars, and heaven. The word אל'הים, Aleim, assists us still less in defining the word God, for Parkhurst translates it as a plural noun signifying "the curser," deriving it from the verb אל'ה (Ale) *to curse*. Finding that philology aids us but little, we must endeavour to arrive at the meaning of the word

"God" by another rule. It is utterly impossible to fix the period of the rise of Theism amongst any particular people, but it is notwithstanding comparatively easy, if not to trace out the development of Theistic ideas, at any rate to point to their probable course of growth amongst all peoples.

Keightley, in his "Origin of Mythology," says—"Supposing, for the sake of hypothesis, a race of men in a state of total or partial ignorance of Deity, their belief in many gods may have thus commenced. They saw around them various changes brought about by human agency, and hence they knew the power of intelligence to produce effects. When they beheld other and greater effects, they ascribed them to some unseen being, similar but superior to man." They associated particular events with special unknown beings (gods), to each of whom they ascribed either a peculiarity of power, or a sphere of action not common to other gods. Thus one was god of the sea, another god of war, another god of love, another ruled the thunder and lightning; and thus through the various elements of the universe and passions of humankind, so far as they were then known.

This mythology became modified with the advancement of human knowledge. The ability to think has proved itself oppugnant to and destructive of the desire to worship. Science has razed altar after altar heretofore erected to the unknown gods, and pulled down deity after deity from the pedestals on which ignorance and superstition had erected them. The priest who had formerly spoken the oracle of God lost his sway, just in proportion as the scientific teacher succeeded in impressing mankind with a knowledge of the facts around them. The ignorant who had hitherto listened unquestioning during centuries of abject submission to their spiritual preceptors, at last commenced to search and examine for themselves, and were guided by experience rather than by church doctrine. To-day it is that advancing intellect challenges the reserve guard of the old armies of superstition, and compels a conflict in which humankind must in the end have great gain by the forced enunciation of the truth.

From the word "God" the Theist derives no argument in his favour; it teaches nothing, defines nothing, demonstrates nothing, explains nothing. The Theist answers that this is no sufficient objection, that there are many words which are in common use to which the same objection applies. Even admitting that this were true, it does not answer the Atheist's objection. Alleging a difficulty on the one side, is not a removal of the obstacle already pointed out on the other.

The Theist declares his God to be not only immutable, but also infinitely intelligent, and says:— "Matter is either essentially intelligent, or essentially non-intelligent; if matter were essentially intelligent, no matter could be without intelligence; but matter cannot be essentially intelligent, because some matter is not intelligent, therefore matter is essentially non-intelligent: but there is intelligence, therefore there must be a cause for the intelligence, independent of matter—this must be an intelligent being—*i.e.*, God." The Atheist answers, I do not know what is meant, in the mouth of the Theist, by "matter." "Matter," "substance," "existence," are three words having the same signification in the Atheist's vocabulary. It is not certain that the Theist expresses any very clear idea when he uses the words "matter" and "intelligence.' Reason and understanding are sometimes treated as separate faculties, yet it is not unfair to presume that the Theist would include them both under the word intelligence. Perception is the foundation of the intellect. The perceptive faculty, or perceptive faculties, differs or differ in each animal: yet in speaking of matter the Theist uses the word "intelligence" as though the same meaning were to be understood in every case. The recollection of the perceptions is the exercise of a different faculty from the perceptive faculty, and occasionally varies disproportionately; thus an individual may have great perceptive faculties, and very little memory, or the reverse—yet memory, as well as perception, is included in intelligence. So also the faculty for comparing between two or more perceptions; the faculty of judging and the faculty of reflecting—all these are subject to the same remarks, and all these and other faculties are included in the word intelligence. We answer, then, that "God" (whatever that word may mean) cannot be intelligent. He can never perceive; the act of perception results in the obtaining a new idea, but if God be omniscient, his ideas have been eternally the same. He has either been always, and always will be perceiving, or he has never perceived at all. But God cannot have been always perceiving, because if he had he would always have been obtaining fresh knowledge, in which case he must have some time had less knowledge than now, that is, he would have been less perfect; that is—he would not have been God: he can never recollect or forget, he can never compare, reflect, nor judge. There cannot be perfect intelligence without understanding; but following Coleridge, "understanding is the faculty of judging according to sense." The faculty of whom? Of some person, judging according to that person's senses? But has "God" senses? Is there anything beyond "God" for "God" to sensate? There cannot be perfect intelligence without reason. By reason we mean that faculty or aggregation of faculties which avails itself of past experience to predetermine, more or less accurately, experience in the future, and to affirm truths which sense perceives, experiment verifies, and experience confirms. To God there can be neither past nor future, therefore to him reason is impossible. There cannot be perfect intelligence without will, but has God will? If God wills, the will of the all-powerful must be irresistible; the will of the infinite must exclude all other wills.

God can never perceive. Perception and sensation are identical. Every sensation is accompanied by pleasure or pain. But God, if immutable, can neither be pleased nor pained. Every fresh sensation involves a change in mental and perhaps in physical condition. God, if immutable, cannot change. Sensation is the source of all ideas, but it is only objects external to the mind which can be sensated. If God be infinite there can be no objects external to him, and therefore sensation must be to him impossible. Yet without perception where is intelligence?

God cannot have memory or reason—memory is of the past, reason for the future, but to God immutable there can be no past, no future. The words past, present, and future imply change; they assert progression of duration. If God be immutable, to him change is impossible. Can you have intelligence destitute of perception, memory, and reason? God cannot have the faculty of judgment—judgment implies in the act of judging a conjoining or disjoining of two or more thoughts, but this involves change of mental condition. To God the immutable, change is impossible. Can you have intelligence, yet no perception, no memory, no reason, no judgment? God cannot think. The law of the thinkable is, that the thing thought must be separated from the thing which is not thought. To think otherwise would be to think of nothing—to have an impression with no distinguishing mark, would be to have no impression. Yet this separation implies change, and to God, immutable, change is impossible. Can you have intelligence without thought? If the Theist replies to this, that he does not mean by infinite intelligence as an attribute of Deity, an infinity of the intelligence found in a finite degree in humankind, then he is bound to explain, clearly and distinctly, what other "intelligence" he means, and until this be done the foregoing statements require answer.

The Atheist does not regard "substance" as either essentially intelligent or the reverse. Intelligence is the result of certain conditions of existence. Burnished steel is bright—that is, brightness is the necessity of a certain condition of existence. Alter the condition, and the characteristic of the condition no longer exists. The only essential of substance is its existence. Alter the wording of the Theist's objection. Matter is either essentially bright, or essentially non-bright. If matter were essentially bright, brightness should be the essence of all matter; but matter cannot be essentially bright, because some matter is not bright, therefore matter is essentially non-bright; but there is brightness, therefore there must be a cause for this brightness independent of matter—that is, there must be an essentially bright being—*i.e.*, God.

Another Theistic proposition is thus stated:—"Every effect must have a cause; the first cause universal must be eternal: *ergo*, the first cause universal must be God." This is equivalent to saying that "God" is "first cause." But what is to be understood by cause? Defined in the absolute, the word has no real value. "Cause," therefore, cannot be eternal. What can be understood by "first cause?" To us the two words convey no meaning greater than would be conveyed by the phrase "round triangle." Cause and effect are correlative terms—each cause is the effect of some precedent; each effect the cause of its consequent. It is impossible to conceive existence terminated by a primal or initial cause. The "beginning," as it is phrased, of the universe, is not thought out by the Theist, but conceded without thought. To adopt the language of Montaigne, "Men make themselves believe that they believe." The so-called belief in Creation is nothing more than the prostration of the intellect on the threshold of the unknown. We can only cognise the ever-succeeding phenomena of existence as a line in continuous and eternal evolution. This line has to us no beginning; we trace it back into the misty regions of the past but a little way, and however far we may be able to journey, there is still the great beyond. Then what is meant by "universal cause?" Spinoza gives the following definition of cause, as used in its absolute signification, "By cause of itself I understand that, the essence of which involves existence, or that, the nature of which can only be considered as existent." That is, Spinoza treats "cause" absolute and "existence" as two words having the same meaning. If his mode of defining the word be contested, then it has no meaning other than its relative signification of a means to an end. "Every effect must have a cause." Every effect implies the plurality of effects, and necessarily that each effect must be finite; but how is it possible from a finite effect to logically deduce an universal—*i.e.*, infinite cause?

There are two modes of argument presented by Theists, and by which, separately or combined, they seek to demonstrate the being of a God. These are familiarly known as the arguments *a priori* and *a posteriori*.

The *a posteriori* argument has been popularised in England by Paley, who has ably endeavoured to hide the weakness of his demonstration under an abundance of irrelevant illustrations. The reasoning of Paley is very deficient in the essential points where it most needed strength. It is utterly impossible to prove by it the eternity or infinity of Deity. As an argument founded on analogy, the design argument, at the best, could only entitle its propounder to infer the existence of a finite cause, or rather of a multitude of finite causes. It ought not to be forgotten that the illustrations of the eye, the watch, and the man, even if admitted as instances of design, or rather of adaptation, are instances of eyes, watches, and men, designed or adapted out of pre-existing substance, by a being of the same kind of substance, and afford, therefore, no demonstration in favour of a designer, alleged to have actually created substance out of nothing, and also alleged to have created a substance entirely different from himself.

The *a posteriori* argument can never demonstrate infinity for Deity. Arguing from an effect finite in extent, the most it could afford would be a cause sufficient for that effect, such cause being possibly finite in extent and duration. And as the argument does not demonstrate God's infinity, neither can it, for the same reason, make out his omniscience, as it is clearly impossible to logically claim infinite wisdom for a God possibly only finite. God's omnipotence remains unproved for the same reason, and because it is clearly absurd to argue that God exercises power where he may not be. Nor can the *a posteriori* argument show God's absolute freedom, for as it does nothing more than seek to prove a finite God, it is quite consistent with the argument that God's existence is limited and controlled in a thousand ways. Nor does this argument show that God always existed; at the best the proof is only that some cause, enough for the effect, existed before it, but there is no evidence that this cause differs from any other causes, which are often as transient as the effect itself. And as it does not demonstrate that God has always existed, neither does it demonstrate that he will always exist, or even that he now exists. It is perfectly in accordance with the argument, and with the analogy of cause and effect, that the effect may remain after the cause has ceased to exist. Nor does the argument from design demonstrate one God. It is quite consistent with this argument that a separate cause existed for each effect, or mark of design discovered, or that several causes contributed to some or one of such effects. So that if the argument be true, it might result in a multitude of petty deities, limited in knowledge, extent, duration, and power; and still worse, each one of this multitude of gods may have had a cause which would also be finite in extent and duration, and would require another, and so on, until the design argument loses the reasoner amongst an innumerable crowd of deities, none of whom can have the attributes claimed for God.

The design argument is defective as an argument from analogy, because it seeks to prove a Creator God who designed, but does not explain whether this God has been eternally designing, which would be absurd; or, if he at some time commenced to design, what then induced him so to commence. It is illogical, for it seeks to prove an immutable Deity, by demonstrating a mutation on the part of Deity.

It is unnecessary to deal specially with each of the many writers who have used from different stand-points the *a posteriori* form of argument in order to prove the existence of Deity. The objections already stated apply to the whole class; and, although probably each illustration used by the theistic advocate is capable of an elucidation entirely at variance with his argument, the main features of objection are the same. The argument *a posteriori* is a method of proof in which the premises are composed of some position of existing facts, and the conclusion asserts a position antecedent to those facts. The argument is from given effects to their causes. It is one form of this argument which asserts that man has a moral nature, and from this seeks to deduce the existence of a moral governor. This form has the disadvantage that its premises are illusory. In alleging a moral nature for man, the theist overlooks the fact that the moral nature of man differs somewhat in each individual, differs considerably in each nation, and differs entirely in some peoples. It is dependent on organisation and education: these are influenced by climate, food, and mode of life. If the argument from man's nature could demonstrate anything, it would prove a murdering God for the murderer, a lascivious God for the licentious man, a dishonest God for the thief, and so through the various phases of human inclination. The *a priori* arguments are methods of proof in which the matter of the premises exists in the order of conception antecedently to that of the conclusion. The argument is from cause to effect. Amongst the prominent theistic advocates relying upon the *à priori* argument in England are Dr. Samuel Clarke, the Rev. Moses Lowman, and William Gillespie. As this last gentleman condemns his predecessors for having utterly failed to demonstrate God's existence, and, as his own treatise on the "Necessary Existence of God" comes to us certified by the praise of Lord Brougham and the approval of Sir William Hamilton, it is to Mr. William Gillespie that the reader shall be directed.

The propositions are first stated entirely, so that Mr. Gillespie may not complain of misrepresentation:—

1. Infinity of extension is necessarily existing.

2. Infinity of extension is necessarily indivisible.

Corollary.—Infinity of extension is necessarily immovable.

3. There is necessarily a being of infinity of extension.

4. The being of infinity of extension is necessarily of unity and simplicity.

Sub-proposition.—The material universe is finite in extension.

5. There is necessarily but one being of infinity of expansion.

Part 2, Proposition 1.—Infinity of duration is necessarily existing.

2. Infinity of duration is necessarily indivisible.

Corollary.—Infinity of duration is necessarily immovable.

3. There is necessarily a being of infinity of duration.

4. The being of infinity of duration is necessarily of unity and simplicity.

Sub-proposition.—The material universe is finite in duration.

Corollary.—Every succession of substances is finite in duration.

5. There is necessarily but one being of infinity of duration.

Part 3, Proposition 1.—There is necessarily a being of infinity of expansion and infinity of duration.

2. The being of infinity of expansion and infinity of duration is necessarily of unity and simplicity.

Division 2, *Part* 1.—The simple sole being of infinity of expansion and of duration is necessarily intelligent and all-knowing.

Part 2.—The simple sole being of infinity of expansion and of duration, who is all-knowing, is necessarily all-powerful.

Part 3.—The simple sole being of infinity of expansion and of duration, who is all-knowing and all-powerful, is necessarily entirely free.

Division 3.—The simple sole being of infinity of expansion and of duration, who is all-knowing, all-powerful, and entirely free, is necessarily completely happy.

Sub-proposition.—The simple sole being of infinity of expansion and of duration, who is all-knowing, all-powerful, entirely free, and completely happy, is necessarily perfectly good.

The first objection against the foregoing argument is, that it seeks to prove too much. It affirms one existence (God) infinite in extent and duration, and another entirely different and distinct existence (the material universe) finite in extent and duration. It therefore seeks to substantiate everything and something more. The first proposition is curiously worded, and the argument to demonstrate it is undoubtedly open to more than one objection.

Mr. Gillespie has not defined infinity, and it is possible therefore his argument may be misapprehended in this paper. Infinite signifies nothing more than indefinite. When a person speaks of infinite extension he can only mean to refer to the extension of something to which he has been unable to set limits. The mind cannot conceive extension *per se*, either absolute or finite. It can only conceive something extended. It might be impossible mentally to define the extension of some substance. In such a case its extension would be indefinite; or, as Mr. Gillespie uses the word, infinite. No one can therefore possibly have any idea of infinity of extension. Yet it is upon the existence of such an idea, and on the impossibility of getting rid of it, that Mr. Gillespie grounds his first proposition. If the idea does not exist, the argument is destroyed at the first step.

Mr. Gillespie argues that it is utterly beyond the power of the human mind to conceive infinity of extension non-existent. He would have been more correct in asserting that it is utterly beyond the power of the human mind to conceive infinity of extension at all, either existent or non-existent. Extension can only be conceived as quality of substance. It is possible to conceive substance extended. It is impossible in thought to limit the possible extension of substance. Mr. Gillespie having asserted that we cannot but believe that infinity of extension exists, proceeds to declare that it exists necessarily. For, he says, everything the existence of which we cannot but believe, exists necessarily. It is not necessary at present to examine what Mr. Gillespie means by existing necessarily; it is sufficient to have shown that we do not believe in the existence of infinity of extension, although we may and do believe in the existence of substance, to the extension of which we may be unable to set limits. But, says Mr. Gillespie, "everything the existence of which we cannot but believe is necessarily existing." Then as we cannot but believe in the existence of the universe (or, to adopt Mr. Gillespie's phrase, the material universe), the material universe exists necessarily. If by "anything necessarily existing," he means anything the essence of which involves existence, or the nature of which can only be considered as existent, then Mr. Gillespie, by demonstrating the necessary existence of the universe, refutes his own later argument, that God is its creator. Mr. Gillespie's argument, as before remarked, is open to misconception, because he has left us without any definition of some of the most important words he uses. To avoid the same objection, it is necessary to state that by substance or existence I mean that which is in itself and is conceived *per se*—that is, the conception of which does not involve the conception of anything else as antecedent to it. By quality, that by which I cognise any mode of existence. By mode, each cognised condition of existence. Regarding extension as quality of mode of substance, and not as substance itself, it appears absurd to argue that the quality exists otherwise than as quality of mode.

The whole of the propositions following the first are so built upon it, that if it fails they are baseless. The second proposition is, that infinity of extension is necessarily indivisible. In dealing with this proposition, Mr. Gillespie talks of the *parts* of infinity of extension, and winds up by saying that he means parts in the sense of partial consideration only. Now not only is it denied that you can have any idea of infinity of extension, but it is also denied that infinity can be the subject of partial consideration. Mr. Gillespie's whole proof of this proposition is intended to affirm that the parts of infinity of extension are necessarily indivisible from each other. I have already denied the possibility of conceiving infinity in parts; and, indeed, if it were possible to conceive infinity in parts, then that infinity could not be indivisible, for Mr. Gillespie says that, by indivisible, he means indivisible, either really or mentally. Now each part of anything conceived is, in the act of conceiving, mentally separated from, either other parts of, or from the remainder of, the whole of which it is part. It is clearly impossible to have a partial consideration of infinity, because the part considered must be mentally distinguished from the unconsidered remainder, and, in that case, you have, in thought, the part considered finite, and the residue certainly limited, at least, by the extent of the part under consideration.

If any of the foregoing objections are well-founded, they are fatal to Mr. Gillespie's argument.

The argument in favour of the corollary to the second proposition is, that the parts of infinity of extension are necessarily immovable amongst themselves; but if there be no such thing as infinity of extension—that is, if extension be only a quality and not necessarily infinite; if infinite mean only indefiniteness or illimitability, and if infinity cannot have parts, this argument goes for very little. The acceptance of the argument that the parts of infinity of extension are immovable, is rendered difficult when the reader considers Mr. Gillespie's sub-proposition (4), that the parts of the material universe are movable and divisible from each other. He urges that a part of the infinity of extension or of its substratum must penetrate the material universe and every atom of it. But if infinity can have no parts, no part of it can penetrate the material universe. If infinity have parts (which is absurd), and if some part penetrate every atom of the material universe, and if the part so penetrating be immovable, how can the material universe be considered as movable, and yet as penetrated in every atom by immovability? If penetrated be a proper phrase, then, at the moment when the part of infinity was penetrating the material universe, the part of infinity so penetrating must have been in motion. Mr. Gillespie's logic is faulty. Use his own language, and there is either no penetration, or there is no immovability.

In his argument for the fourth proposition, Mr. Gillespie—having by his previous proposition demonstrated (?) what he calls a substratum for the before demonstrated (?) infinity of extension—says, "it is intuitively evident that the substratum of infinity of extension can be no more divisible than infinity of extension." Is this so? Might not a complex and divisible substratum be conceived by us as possible to underlie a (to us) simple and indivisible indefinite extension, if the conception of the latter were possible to us? There cannot be any intuition. It is mere assumption, as, indeed, is the assumption of extension at all, other than as the extension of substance. In his argument for proposition 5, Gillespie says that "any one who asserts that he can suppose two or more necessarily existing beings, each of infinity of expansion, is no more to be argued with than one who denies, Whatever is, is. Why is it more difficult to suppose this than to suppose one being of infinity, and, in addition to this infinity, a material universe? Is it impossible to suppose a necessary being of heat, one of light, and one of electricity, all occupying the same indefinite expansion? If it be replied that you cannot conceive two distinct and different beings occupying the same point at the same moment, then it must be equally impossible to conceive the material universe and God existing together.

The second division of Mr. Gillespie's argument is also open to grave objection. Having demonstrated to his own satisfaction an infinite substance, and also having assumed in addition a finite substance, and having called the first, infinite "being;" perhaps from a devout objection to speak of God as substance, Mr. Gillespie seeks to prove that the infinite being is intelligent. He says, "Intelligence either began to be, or it never began to be. That it never began to be is evident in this, that if it began to be, it must have had a cause; for whatever begins to be must have a cause. And the cause of intelligence must be of intelligence; for what is not of intelligence cannot make intelligence begin to be. Now intelligence being before intelligence began to be, is a contradiction. And this absurdity following from the supposition, that intelligence began to be, it is proved that intelligence never began to be: to wit, is of infinity of duration." Mr. Gillespie does not condescend to tell us why "what is not of intelligence cannot make intelligence begin to be;" but it is not unfair to suppose that he means that of things which have nothing in common one cannot be the cause of the other. Let us apply Mr. Gillespie's argument to the material universe, the existence of which is to him so certain that he has treated it as a self-evident proposition.

The material universe—that is, matter, either began to be, or it never began to be. That it never began to be, is evident in this, that if it began to be, it must have had a cause; for whatever begins to be must have a cause. And the cause of matter, must be of matter; for what is not of matter, cannot make matter begin to be. Now matter being before matter began to be, is a contradiction. And this absurdity following from the supposition that matter—*i.e.*, the material universe, began to be, it is proved that the material universe never began to be—to wit, is of indefinite duration.

The argument as to the eternity of matter is at least as logical as the argument for the eternity of intelligence. Mr. Gillespie may reply, that he affirms the material universe to be finite in duration, and that by the argument for his proposition, part 2, he proves that the one infinite being (God) is the creator of matter. His words are, "As the material universe is finite in duration, or began to be, it must have had a cause; for, whatever begins to be must have a cause. And this cause must be [Mr. Gillespie does not explain why], in one respect or other, the simple sole being of infinity of expansion and duration. who is all-knowing [the all-knowing or intelligence rests on the argument which has just been shown to be equally applicable to matter] inasmuch as what being, or cause independent of that being, could there be? And therefore, that being made matter begin to be." Taking Mr. Gillespie's own argument, that which made matter begin to be, must be of matter, for what is not matter, cannot make matter begin to be; then Mr. Gillespie's infinite being (God) must be matter. But there is yet another exception to the proposition, which is, that the infinite being (God) is all-powerful. Having as above argued that the being made matter, he proceeds, "and this being shown, it must be granted that the being is, necessarily, all-powerful." Nothing of the kind need be granted. If it were true that it was demonstrated that the infinite being (God) made matter, it would not prove him able to make anything else; it might show the being cause enough for that effect, but does not demonstrate him cause for all effects. So that if no better argument can be found to prove God all-powerful, his omnipotence remains unproved.

Mr. Gillespie's last proposition is that the being (God) whose existence he has so satisfactorily (?) made out, is necessarily completely happy. In dealing with this proposition, Mr. Gillespie talks of unhappiness as existing in various kinds and degrees. But, to adopt his own style of argument, Unhappiness either began to be, or it never began to be. That it never began to be is evident in this, that whatever began to be must have had a cause; for whatever begins to be must have a cause. And the cause of unhappiness must be of unhappiness, for what is not of unhappiness cannot make unhappiness begin to be. But unhappiness being before unhappiness began to be, is a contradiction; therefore unhappiness is of infinity of duration. But proposition 5, part 2, says there is but one being of infinity of duration. The one being of infinity of duration is therefore necessarily unhappy. Mr. Gillespie's arguments recoil on himself, and are destructive of his own affirmations.

In his argument for the sub-proposition, Mr. Gillespie says that God's motive, or one of his motives to create, must be believed to have been a desire to make happiness, besides his own consummate happiness, begin to be. That is God, who is consummate happiness everywhere for ever, *desired* something. That is, he wanted more than then existed. That is, his happiness was not complete. That is, Mr. Gillespie refutes himself. But what did infinite and eternal complete happiness desire? It desired (says Mr. Gillespie) to make more happiness—that is, to make more than an infinity of complete happiness. Mr. Gillespie's proof, on the whole, is at most that there exists necessarily substance, the extension and duration of which we cannot limit. Part of his argument involves the use of the very *a posteriori* reasoning justly considered regarded by himself as utterly worthless for the demonstration of the existence of a being with such attributes as orthodox Theism tries to assert.

If Sir William Hamilton meant no flattery in writing that Mr. Gillespie's work was one of the "very ablest" on the Theistic side, how wretched indeed must, in his opinion, have been the logic of the less able advocates for Theism. Every Theist must admit that if a God exists, he could have so convinced all men of the fact of his existence that doubt, disagreement, or disbelief would be impossible. If he could not do this, he would not be omnipotent, or he would not be omniscient—that is, he would not be God. Every Theist must also agree that if a God exists, he would wish all men to have such a clear consciousness of his existence and attributes that doubt, disagreement, or belief on this subject would be impossible. And this, if for no other reason, because that out of doubts and disagreements on religion have too often resulted centuries of persecution, strife, and misery, which a good God would desire to prevent. If God would not desire this, then he is not all-good—that is, he is not God. But as many men have doubts, a large majority of mankind have disagreements, and some men have disbeliefs as to God's existence and attributes; it follows either that God does not exist, or that he is not all-wise, or that he is not all-powerful, or that he is not all-good.

Every child is born into the world an Atheist; and if he grows into a Theist, his Deity differs with the country in which the believer may happen to be born, or the people amongst whom he may happen to be educated. The belief is the result of education or organisation. Religious belief is powerful in proportion to the want of scientific knowledge on the part of the believer. The more ignorant, the more credulous. In the mind of the Theist "God" is equivalent to the sphere of the unknown; by the use of the word he answers without thought problems which might otherwise obtain scientific solution. The more ignorant the Theist, the greater his God. Belief in God is not a faith founded on reason; but a prostration of the reasoning faculties on the threshold of the unknown. Theism is worse than illogical; its teachings are not only without utility, but of itself it has nothing to teach. Separated from Christianity with its almost innumerable sects, from Mahomedanism with its numerous divisions, and separated also from every other preached system, Theism is a Will-o'-the-wisp, without reality. Apart from othodoxy, Theism is a boneless skeleton; the various mythologies give it alike flesh and bone, otherwise coherence it hath none. What does Christian Theism teach? That the first man made perfect by the all-powerful, all-wise, all-good God, was nevertheless imperfect, and by his imperfection brought misery into the world, where the all-good God must have intended misery should never come. That this God made men to share this misery, men whose fault was their being what he made them. That this God begets a son, who is nevertheless his unbegotten self, and that by belief in the birth of God's eternal son, and in the death of the undying who died to satisfy God's vengeance, man may escape the consequences of the first man's error. Christian Theism declares that belief alone can save man, and yet recognises the fact that man's belief results from teaching, by establishing missionary societies to spread the faith. Christian Theism teaches that God, though no respector of persons, selected as his favourites one nation in preference to all others; that man can do no good of himself or without God's aid, but yet that each man has a free will; that God is all-powerful, but that few go to heaven and the majority to hell; that all are to love God, who has predestined from eternity that by far the largest number of human beings are to be burning in hell for ever. Yet the advocates for Theism venture to upraid those who argue against such a faith.

It is not pretended that this inefficient Plea for Atheism contains either a refutation of all or even the majority of Theistic arguments, or that it offers an explanation of every objection against Atheism; but it is hoped that enough is here stated to induce some one of ability on the Theistic side to write for the better instruction of such as entertain the views here advocated—views held sincerely, views propagated actively, and views which are permeating more widely than is generally supposed.

Either Theism is true or false. If true, discussion must help to spread its influence; if false, the sooner it ceases to influence human conduct the better for human kind. It will be useless for the clergy to urge that such a pamphlet deserves no reply. It is true the writer is unimportant, and the language in which his thoughts find expression lacks the polish of a Macaulay, and the fervour of a Burke; but they are nevertheless his thoughts, uttered because it is not only his right, but his duty to give them utterance. And this Plea for Atheism is put forth challenging the Theists to battle for their cause, and in the hope that the strugglers being sincere, truth may give laurels to the victor and the vanquished; laurels to the victor in that he has upheld the truth; laurels still welcome to the vanquished, whose defeat crowns him with a truth he knew not of before.